THE ISLAND OF STATUES

The Island of Statues

An Arcadian Faery Tale—In Two Acts

W. B. Yeats

QUINX BOOKS

First published 1885
This edition published 2014
Introduction © 2014 by Keith Miller
Quinx Books
quinxbooks.com

CONTENTS

INTRODUCTION

by Keith Miller

The Island of Statues was William Butler Yeats' first published work. He wrote it in the early 1880s in Dublin, where he was attending the Metropolitan School of Art, and also spending time in the studio of his father, John ("Jack") Butler Yeats. The elder Yeats was a prominent painter, with connections to many of the city's artists and writers. He read widely, and his literary inclinations strongly influenced his son. In his *Autobiographies*, W. B. Yeats writes: "I had begun to write poetry in imitation of Shelley and of Edmund Spenser, play after play—for my father exalted dramatic poetry above all other kinds—and I invented fantastic and incoherent plots."[1] Among these "fantastic" plays were *Mosada*, Yeats' first standalone publication—his father commissioned a private edition of one hundred copies; *Vivien and Time*; *Love and Death*; and *The Blindness*. The latter two remain unpublished. *The Island of Statues* was, in the estimation of readers of the time and Yeats himself, the most successful of these early works.

Here is Yeats' account in his *Autobiographies* of what was perhaps the first public appearance of the play: "I had been invited to read out a poem called 'The Island of Statues,' an Arcadian play in imitation of Edmund Spenser, to a gathering of critics who were to decide whether it was worthy of publication in the College magazine. The magazine had already published a lyric of mine, the first ever printed, and people began to know my name. We met in the rooms of Mr. C. H. Oldham, now professor of Political Economy at our new University; and though Professor Bury, then a very young man, was to be the deciding voice, Mr. Oldham had asked quite a large audience. When the reading was over and the poem had been approved I was left alone, why I cannot remember, with a young man who was, I had been told, a school-master. I was silent, gathering my courage, and he also was silent; and presently I said without anything to lead up to it, 'I know you will defend the ordinary system of education by saying that it strengthens the will, but I am convinced that it only seems to do so because it weakens the impulses.' Then I stopped, overtaken by shyness. He made no answer but smiled and looked surprised as though I had said, 'you will say they are Persian attire; but let them be changed.'"[2] Two poems from the play, "Song of the Faeries" and "Voices," appeared in the March 1885 issue of the *Dublin University Review*, and the entire play was serialized from April through July 1885.

The Island of Statues clearly held a place of importance for Yeats. When his first conventionally published volume of poetry, *The Wanderings of Oisin and Other Poems*, came out in 1889, he was dismayed that the full play could not be included. Writing to a friend, he said: "I am sorry that the whole of 'The Island of Statues' is not in my book. It would have increased the book in size too much. It will be printed later on in some future volume."[3] (The play was in fact never printed in its entirety until the present volume.) When in 1933 Yeats put together his *Collected Poems*, he began with "The Song of the Happy Shepherd," which was first published in the *Dublin University Review* as "An Epilogue to the 'Island of Statues' and 'The Seeker,'" thus indicating the foundational status of the work. Both *The Seeker* and "The Song of the Happy Shepherd" are included at the end of this volume.

The Island of Statues was to impact Yeats' life in another way. Maud Gonne, the beautiful and vivacious Irish revolutionary, read the play in the *Dublin University Review* and fell in love with it. Here is Yeats' account of their first meeting: "Miss Gonne (you have heard of her, no doubt) was here yesterday with introduction from the O'Learys; she says she cried over 'Island of Statues' fragment, but altogether favored the Enchantress and hated Na[s]china."[4] Gonne was to become Yeats' obsession and muse for years, though his love for her remained unrequited until 1908.

The obvious influences on the play are Spenser's *The Faerie Queene* and three works by Percy Bysshe Shelley: *Prometheus Unbound* (a touchstone work for Yeats), *Alastor*, and *The Witch of Atlas*. In a BBC interview in 1938, Yeats also mentioned Keats and Ben Jonson as influences. Two subtler influences are *The Maid's Tragedy* (1619) by Francis Beaumont and John Fletcher, from which Yeats apparently lifted the name Amintor (becoming "Almintor" in *Statues*), and Irish dramatist Richard Lalor Sheil's *Evadne; or, The Statue* (1819). Naschina was Evadne in early versions of the play.[5]

Yeats was influenced not only by the Romantics, but by the Pre-Raphaelite Brotherhood, whose works embraced mythology and rich, exotic detail. His father had become involved with the movement, and even moved into a Pre-Raphaelite–inspired community at one point. The young Yeats took part in weekly debates at the house of William Morris, and later declared: "I was in all things Pre-Raphaelite."[6]

The Pre-Raphaelites and what they stood for fell out of favor in the early 1900s, displaced by modernism. The early works of Yeats, like the early stories of E. M. Forster, were disparaged, considered by critics to be misguided mystical juvenilia. However, the influence of *The Island of Statues* on Yeats' later work is obvious. In particular, his lifelong exploration of antimonies—nature versus art, time versus eternity, the self versus the mask—starts to take shape in the play. It should be noted as well that, late in life, Yeats returned to his mystical beginnings. Indeed, the ominous atmosphere of "The Second Coming" and the esoteric, occult-inspired *The Vision* owes much to Yeats' early obsession with enchantment and magical destinies.

The sumptuous delights of the Pre-Raphaelites were rediscovered in the 1960s, at a time when the similarly fantastical, myth-inspired works of Tolkien were being celebrated. Their rehabilitation culminated in a key 1984 exhibition at the Tate Gallery in London. The paintings of Lord Leighton, John William Waterhouse, and Dante Gabriel Rossetti have been returned to their rightful place in the pantheon. It is time that the early mythical-mystical achievements of Yeats received the same recognition.

NOTES

1. Yeats, W. B. 1966. *Autobiographies*. London: Macmillan, 66–67.
2. *Autobiographies*, 92–93.
3. Finneran, Richard J., George Mills Harper, and William M. Murphy, eds. *Letters to W. B. Yeats*. 1977. New York: Columbia University Press. Vol. 1:4.
4. *Letters to W. B. Yeats*, Vol 1:106.
5. Yeats, W. B. 1987. *The Early Poetry*. Vol. 1: *Mosada* and *The Island of Statues*. George Bornstein, ed. Ithaca, NY: Cornell University Press.
6. *Autobiographies*, 76.

THE ISLAND OF STATUES

An Arcadian Faery Tale—In Two Acts

Dramatis Personæ

NASCHINA—*Shepherdess*

COLIN—*Shepherd*

THERNOT—*Shepherd*

ALMINTOR—*A hunter*

ANTONIO—*His page*

ENCHANTRESS OF THE ISLAND

And a company of the Sleepers of the Isle.

ACT I

SCENE I

Before the cottage of NASCHINA. *It is morning, and away in the depth of the heaven the moon is fading.*

Enter THERNOT *with a lute.*

THERNOT: Maiden, come forth: the woods keep watch for thee;
　　Within the drowsy blossom hangs the bee;
　　'Tis morn: thy sheep are wandering down the vale—
　　'Tis morn: like old men's eyes the stars are pale,
　　And thro' the odorous air love-dreams are winging—

'Tis morn, and from the dew-drench'd wood I've sped

To welcome thee, Naschina, with sweet singing.

> [*Sitting on a tree-stem, he begins to tune his lute.*

Enter COLIN, *abstractedly.*

COLIN: Come forth: the morn is fair; as from the pyre

    Of sad Queen Dido shone the lapping fire

    Unto the wanderers' ships, or as the day fills

    The brazen sky, so blaze the daffodils;

    As Argive Clytemnestra saw out-burn

    The flagrant signal of her lord's return

    Afar, clear-shining on the herald hills,

    In vale and dell so blaze the daffodils;

    As when upon her cloud-o'er-muffled steep

    Œnone saw the fires of Troia leap,

    And laugh'd, so, so along the bubbling rills

    In lemon-tinted lines, so blaze the daffodils.

    Come forth, come forth, my music flows for thee,

    A quenchless grieving of love melody.

> [*Raises his lute.*

THERNOT [*Sings*]: Now her sheep all browsing meet

    By the singing waters' edge,

    Tread and tread their cloven feet

    On the ruddy river sedge,

For the dawn the foliage fingereth,

    And the waves are leaping white,

She alone, my lady, lingereth

    While the world is roll'd in light.

COLIN: Shepherd, to mar the morning hast thou come?

Hear me, and, shepherd, hearing me grow dumb.

[*Sings*] Where is the owl that lately flew

    Flickering under the white moonshine?

She sleeps with owlets two and two

    Sleepily close her round bright eyne:

O'er her nest the lights are blending:

    Come thou, come, and to this string—

Though my love-sick heart is rending,

    Not a sad note will I sing.

THERNOT: I am not dumb: I'd sooner silent wait

Within the fold to hear the creaking gate—

[*Sings*] The wood and the valley and sea

    Awaken, awaken to new-born luster;

A new day's troop of wasp and bee

    Hang on the side of the round grape cluster;

Blenching on high the dull stars sicken

    Morn bewildered, and the cup

Of the tarn where young waves quicken

    Hurls their swooning lustre up.

COLIN: I'll silence this dull singer—

[*Sings*] Oh, more dark thy gleaming hair is
   Than the peeping pansy's face,
  And thine eyes more bright than faery's,
   Dancing in some moony place,
  And thy neck's a poisèd lily;
   See I tell thy beauties o'er,
  As within a cellar chilly
   Some old miser tells his store;
  And thy memory I keep,
   Till all else is empty chaff,
  Till I laugh when others weep,
   Weeping when all others laugh.

THERNOT: I'll quench his singing with loud song—
[*Sings wildly*] Come forth, for in a thousand bowers
   Blossoms open dewy lips;
  Over the lake the water-flowers
   Drift and float like silver ships;
  Ever ringing, ringing, ringing,
   With unfaltering persistence,
  Hundred-throated morn is singing,
   Joy and love are one existence.

COLIN: [*Sings*] Lone, and wanting thee, I weep;
   Love and sorrow, one existence,
  Sadness, soul of joy most deep,
   Is the burthen and persistence

Of the songs that never sleep.

Love from heaven came of yore

As a token and a sign,

Singing o'er and o'er and o'er

Of his death and change malign.

THERNOT: With fiery song I'll drown yon puny voice.

[*Leaping to his feet.*

[*Sings*] Passeth the moon with her sickle of light,

Slowly, slowly fadeth she,

Weary of reaping the barren night

And the desolate shuddering sea.

COLIN: [*Sings*] Loud for thee the morning crieth,

And my soul in waiting dieth,

Ever dieth, dieth, dieth.

THERNOT: [*Sings*] Far the morning vapours shatter,

As the leaves in autumn scatter.

COLIN: [*Sings*] In the heart of the dawn the rivers are singing,

Over them crimson vapours winging.

THERNOT: [*Sings*] All the world is ringing, ringing;

All the world is singing, singing.

COLIN: [*Sings*] Lift my soul from rayless night—

THERNOT: [*Sings*] Stricken all the night is past—

COLIN: [*Sings*] Music of my soul and light—

THERNOT [*Sings*] Back the shadows creep aghast—

[*They approach one another, while singing, with angry gestures.*

Enter NASCHINA.

NASCHINA: O cease your singing! wild and shrill and loud,
  On my poor brain your busy tumults crowd.

COLIN: I fain had been the first of singing things
  To welcome thee, when o'er the owlet's wings
  And troubled eyes came morning's first-born glow;
  But yonder thing, yon idle noise, yon crow,
  Yon shepherd—

THERNOT: Came your spirit to beguile
  With singing sweet as e'er round lake-lulled isle
  Sing summer waves. But yonder shepherd vile
  All clamour-clothed—

COLIN: Was't clamour when *I* sung
  Whom men have named Arcadia's sweetest tongue.

                    [*A horn sounds.*

  A horn! some troop of robbers winding goes
  Along the wood with subtle tread and bended bows.

                    [*An arrow passes above.*

  Fly!

THERNOT: Fly!

                    [COLIN *and* THERNOT *go.*

NASCHINA: So these brave shepherds both are gone.
  Courageous miracles!

Enter ALMINTOR *and* ANTONIO, *talking together.*

ALMINTOR: The sunlight shone
　　　Upon his wings. Thro' yonder green abyss
　　　I sent an arrow.

ANTONIO:　　　And I saw you miss;
　　　And far away the heron sails, I wis.

ALMINTOR: Nay, nay, I miss'd him not; his days
　　　Of flight are done.

　　　　　　　　　[*Seeing* NASCHINA *and bowing low.*

　　　Most fair of all who graze
　　　Their sheep in Arcady, Naschina, hail!
　　　Naschina, hail!

ANTONIO [*Mimicking him*]:　　Most fair of all who graze
　　　Their sheep in Arcady, Naschina, hail!
　　　Naschina, hail!

ALMINTOR:　　I'd drive thy woolly sheep,
　　　If so I might, along a dewy vale,
　　　Where all night long the heavens weep and weep,
　　　Dreaming in their soft odour-laden sleep,
　　　Where all night long the lonely moon, the white
　　　Sad Lady of the deep, pours down her light;
　　　And 'mong the stunted ash-trees' drooping rings,
　　　All flame-like gushing from the hollow stones,
　　　By day and night a lonely fountain sings,

And there to its own heart for ever moans.

NASCHINA: I'd be alone.

ALMINTOR: We two, by that pale fount,

Unmindful of its woes would twine a wreath

As fair as any that on Ida's mount

Long ere an arrow whizzed or sword left sheath

The shepherd Paris for Œnone made,

Singing of arms and battles some old stave,

As lies dark water in a murmurous glade,

Dreaming the live-long summer in the shade,

Dreaming of flashing flight and of the pluméd wave.

ANTONIO: Naschina, wherefore are your eyes so bright

With tears?

NASCHINA: I weary of ye. There is none

Of all on whom Arcadian suns have shone

Sustains his soul in courage or in might.

Poor race of leafy Arcady, your love

To prove what can ye do? What things above

Sheep-guiding, or the bringing some strange bird,

Or some small beast most wonderfully furr'd,

Or sad sea-shells where little echoes sit?

Such quests as these, I trow, need little wit.

ANTONIO: And the great grey lynx's skin.

NASCHINA: In sooth, methinks

That I myself could shoot a great grey lynx.

[NASCHINA *turns to go.*

23

ALMINTOR: Oh stay, Naschina, stay!

NASCHINA: Here, where men know the gracious woodland joys,
    Joy's brother, Fear, dwells ever in each breast—
    Joy's brother, Fear, lurks in each leafy way.
    I weary of your songs and hunter's toys.
    To prove his love a knight with lance in rest
    Will circle round the world upon a quest,
    Until afar appear the gleaming dragon-scales:
    From morn the twain until the evening pales
    Will struggle. Or he'll seek enchanter old,
    Who sits in lonely splendour mail'd in gold,
    And they will war, 'mid wondrous elfin-sights:
    Such may I love. The shuddering forest lights
    Of green Arcadia do not hide, I trow,
    Such men, such hearts. But, uncouth hunter, thou
    Know'st naught of this.

                                     [She goes.

ANTONIO: And, uncouth hunter, now—

ALMINTOR: Ay, boy.

ANTONIO: Let's see if that same heron's dead.

        [The boy runs out, followed slowly by ALMINTOR.

(END OF SCENE I)

Scene II

Sundown.—A remote forest valley.

Enter ALMINTOR, *followed by* ANTONIO.

ANTONIO: And whither uncouth hunter? Why so fast?

    So I 'mid the willow-glade you pause at last.

ALMINTOR: Here is the place, the cliff-encircled wood;

    Here grow that shy, retiring sisterhood,

    The pale anemones. We've sought all day,

    And found.

ALMINTOR: 'Tis well! another mile of way

    I could not go.

                          [*They sit down.*

ALMINTOR: Let's talk, and let's be sad,

    Here in the shade.

ANTONIO: Why? Why?

ALMINTOR: For what is glad?

    For, look you, sad's the murmur of the bees,

    Yon wind goes sadly and the grass and trees

    Reply like moaning of imprisoned elf:

The whole world's sadly talking to itself.
The waves in yonder lake where points my hand
Beat out their lives lamenting o'er the sand;
The birds that nestle in the leaves are sad,
Poor sad wood-rhapsodists.

ANTONIO: Not so: they're glad.

ALMINTOR: All rhapsody hath sorrow for its soul.

ANTONIO: Yon eager lark, that fills with song the whole
Of this wide vale, embosomed in the air,
Is sorrow in his song, or any care?
Doth not yon bird, yon quivering bird, rejoice?

ALMINTOR: I hear the whole sky's sorrow in one voice.

ANTONIO: Nay, nay, Almintor, yonder song is glad.

ALMINTOR: 'Tis beautiful, and therefore it is sad.

ANTONIO: Have done this phrasing, and say why, in sooth,
Almintor, thou hast grown so full of ruth,
And wherefore have we come?

ALMINTOR: A song to hear.

ANTONIO: But whence, and when?

ALMINTOR: Over the willows sere
Out of the air.

ANTONIO: And when?

ALMINTOR: When the sun goes down
Over the crown of the willows brown.
Oh, boy, I'm bound on a most fearful quest;
For so she willed thou heard'st? Upon the breast

26

Of yonder lake from whose green banks alway
The poplars gaze across the waters grey,
And nod to one another, lies a green,
Small island where the full soft sheen
Of evening and glad silence dwelleth aye,
For there the great Enchantress lives.

ANTONIO: And there
Groweth the goblin flower of joy, her care,
By many sought, and 'tis a forest tale,
How they who seek are ever doomed to fail.
Some say that all who touch the island lone
Are changed for ever into moon-white stone.

ALMINTOR: That flower I seek.

ANTONIO: Thou never wilt return.

ALMINTOR: I'll bring that flower to her, and so may earn
Her love: to her who wears that bloom comes truth,
And elvish wisdom, and long years of youth
Beyond a mortal's years. I wait the song
That calls.

ANTONIO: O evil starred!

ALMINTOR: It comes along
The wind at evening when the sun goes down
Over the crown of the willows brown.
See, yonder sinks the sun, yonder a shade
Goes flickering in reverberated light.
There! There! Dost thou not see?

ANTONIO: I see the night,

Deep-eyed, slow-footing down the empty glade.

A VOICE [*sings*]: From the shadowy hollow

Arise thou and follow!

ALMINTOR: Sad faery tones.

ANTONIO: 'Tis thus they ever seem,

As some dead maiden's singing in a dream.

VOICE: When the tree was o'er-appled

For mother Eve's winning

I was at her sinning.

O'er the grass light-endappled

I wandered and trod,

O'er the green Eden-sod

And I sang round the tree

As I sing now to thee:

Arise from the hollow

And follow, and follow!

Away in the green paradise,

As I wandered unseen,

(How glad was her mien!),

I saw her as you now arise;

Before her I trod

O'er the green Eden-sod,

And I sang round the tree,

As I sing now to thee:

From the shadowy hollow

Come follow! Come follow!

[ALMINTOR *goes.*

[*The Voice sings, dying away*]

And I sang round the tree,

As I sing now to thee:

From the green shaded hollow

Arise, worm, and follow!

ANTONIO: I too will follow for this evil-starred one's sake

Unto the dolorous border of the fairy lake.

[ANTONIO *goes.*

(END OF SCENE II)

Scene III

THE BIRTH OF NIGHT. —THE ISLAND. *Far into the distance reach shadowy ways, burdened with faery flowers. Knee-deep amongst them stand the immovable figures of those who have failed in their quest.*

FIRST VOICE: See! oh see! the dew-drowned bunches
      Of the monk's-hood how they shake,
      Nodding by the flickering lake,
    There where yonder squirrel crunches
      Acorns green with eyes awake.
SECOND VOICE: I followed him from my green lair,
      But wide awake his two eyes were.
FIRST VOICE: Oh, learnèd is each monk's-hood's mind,
      And full of wisdom is each bloom,
      As clothed in ceremonial gloom,
    They hear the story of the wind,
      That dieth slow with sunsick doom.
SECOND VOICE: The south breeze now in dying fears
      Tells all his sinning in their ears.

FIRST VOICE: He says 'twas he and 'twas no other,

    Blew my crimson cap away

    O'er the lake this very day.

  Hark! he's dead—my drowsy brother

    And has not heard. *Absolvo te.*

                             [A pause.

FIRST VOICE: Peace, peace, the earth's a-quake. I hear

    Some barbarous, un-faery thing draw near.

Enter ALMINTOR.

ALMINTOR: The evening gleams are green and gold and red

    Along the lake. The crane has homeward fled.

    And flowers around in clustering thousands are,

    Each shining clear as some unbaffled star;

    The skies more dim, though burning like a shield,

    Above these men whose mouths were sealed

    Long years ago, and unto stone congealed.

    And oh! the wonder of the thing! each came

    When low the sun sank down in clotted flame

    Beyond the lake, whose smallest wave was burdened

    With rolling fire, beyond the high trees turbaned

    With clinging mist, each star-fought wanderer came

    As I, to choose beneath day's dying flame;

    And they are all now stone as I shall be

Unless some pitying god shall succour me
In this my choice.

[*Stoops over a flower, then pauses.*

Some god might help; if so
Mayhap 'twere better that aside I throw
All choice, and give to chance for guiding chance
Some cast of die, or let some arrow glance
For guiding of the gods. The sacred bloom
To seek not hopeless have I crossed the gloom,
With that song leading where harmonic woods
Nourish the panthers in dim solitudes;
Vast greenness where eternal Rumour dwells,
And hath her home by many-folded dells.
I passed by many caves of dripping stone,
And heard each unseen Echo on her throne,
Lone regent of the woods, deep muttering,
And then new murmurs came new uttering
In song from goblin waters swaying white,
Mocking with patient laughter all the night
Of those vast woods; and then I saw the boat,
Living, wide wingèd, on the waters float.
Strange draperies did all the sides adorn,
And the waves bowed before it like mown corn,
The wingèd wonder of all Faery Land.
It bore me softly where the shallow sand
Binds as within a girdle or a ring,

The lake-embosomed isle. Nay, this my quest
Shall not so hopeless prove: some god may rest
Upon the wind and guide mine arrow's course.
From yonder pinnacle above the lake
I'll send mine arrow, now my one resource;
The nighest blossom where it falls I'll take.

       [Goes out, fitting an arrow to his bow.

A VOICE: Fickle the guiding his arrow shall find!
    Some goblin my servant on wings that are fleet,
        That nestles alone in the whistling wind,
    Go pilot the course of his arrow's deceit!

       [The arrow falls.

Re-enter ALMINTOR.

ALMINTOR: 'Tis here the arrow fell: the breezes laughed
    Around the feathery tip. Unto the shaft
    This blossom is most near. Statue! Oh thou
    Whose beard a moonlight river is, whose brow
    Is stone: old sleeper! this same afternoon
    O'er much I've talked: I shall be silent soon,
    If wrong my choice, as silent as thou art.
    Oh! gracious Pan, take new thy servant's part.
    He was our ancient god. If I speak low,
    And not too clear, how will the new god know

But that I called on him?

> [*Pulls the flower and becomes stone. From among the*
> *flowers a sound as of a multitude of horns.*

A VOICE: Sleeping lord of archery,

> No more a-roving shalt thou see
> The panther with her yellow hide,
> Of the forests all the pride,
> Or her ever burning eyes,
> When she in a cavern lies,
> Watching o'er her awful young,
> Where their sinewy might is strung
> In the never-lifting dark.
> No! Thou standest still and stark,
> That of old wert moving ever,
> But a mother panther never
> O'er her young so eagerly
> Did her lonely watching take
> As I my watching lest you wake,
> Sleeping lord of archery.

(END OF SCENE II)

ACT II

SCENE I

The wood in the early evening. Enter ANTONIO *and* NASCHINA.

NASCHINA: I as a shepherd dressed will seek and seek
    Until I find him. What a weary week,
    My pretty child, since he has gone, oh say
    Once more how on that miserable day
    He passed across the lake.

ANTONIO: When we two came
    From the wood's ways, then, like a silver flame
    We saw the dolorous lake; and then thy name
    He carved on trees and with a sun-dry weed
    He wrote it on the sands (the owls may read
    And ponder it if they will); then near at hand
    The boat's prow grated on the shallow sand,

And loudly twice the living wings flapt wide,
And leaping to their feet, far Echoes cried,
Each other answering. Then between each wing
He sat, and then I heard the white lake sing,
Curving beneath the prow; as some wild drake
Half lit, so flapt the wings across the lake—
Alas! I make you sadder, shepherdess.

NASCHINA: Nay, grief in feeding on old grief grows less.

ANTONIO: Grief needs much feeding then. Of him I swear
We've talked and talked, and not a whit more rare
Your weeping fits!

NASCHINA: Look you, so very strait
The barred woodpecker's mansion is and deep,
No other bird may enter in.

ANTONIO: Well?

NASCHINA: Late—
Aye, very lately, sorrow came to weep
Within mine heart; and naught but sorrow now
Can enter there.

ANTONIO: See! See! above yon brow
Of hill two shepherds come.

NASCHINA: Farewell! I'll don
My shepherd garments, and return anon.

                                        [*Goes.*

36

Enter COLIN *and* THERNOT.

THERNOT: Two men who love one maid have ample cause
    Of war. Of yore, two shepherds, where we pause,
    Fought once for self-same reason on the hem
    Of the wide woods.

COLIN: And the deep earth gathered them.

THERNOT: We must get swords.

COLIN: Is't the only way? Oh, see,
    Yon is the hunter's, Sir Almintor's, page;
    Let him between us judge, for he can gauge
    And measure out the ways of chivalry.

THERNOT: Sir Page, Almintor's friend, and therefore learned
    In all such things, pray let thine ears be turned,
    And hear and judge.

ANTONIO: My popinjay, what now?

COLIN: This thing we ask: must we two fight? Judge thou.
    Each came one morn, with welcoming of song,
    Unto her door; for this, where nod the long
    And shoreward waves, we nigh have fought; waves bring
    The brown weed burden, so the sword brings fear
    To us.

THERNOT: Oh wise art thou in such a thing,
    Being Almintor's page. Now judge you here.
    We love Naschina both.

ANTONIO: Whom loves *she* best?

COLIN: She cares no whit for either, but has blest
    Almintor with her love.

Enter NASCHINA, *disguised as a shepherd.*

COLIN: Who art thou?—speak,
    As the sea's furrows on a sea-tost shell,
    Sad histories are lettered on thy cheek.
ANTONIO: It is the shepherd Guarimond, who loveth well
    In the deep centres of the secret woods.
    Old miser hoards of grief to tell and tell:
    Young Guarimond he tells them o'er and o'er,
    To see them drowned by those vast solitudes,
    With their unhuman sorrows.
NASCHINA: Cease! no more!
    Thou hast an over-nimble tongue.
COLIN: Thy grief,
    What is it, friend?
ANTONIO: He lost i' the woods the chief
    And only sheep he loved of all the troop.
COLIN: More grief is mine. No man shall ever stoop
    Beneath the weight of greater grief than I;
    I like you, and, in sooth I know not why.
    Now, judge, must shepherd Thernot there and I
    For this thing fight—we love one maid?

NASCHINA: Her name?

COLIN: Naschina.

NASCHINA: Oh, I know her well—a lame,

    Dull-witted thing with face red squirrel-brown.

ANTONIO: A long brown grasshopper of maids!

NASCHINA: Peace, sir!

COLIN: 'Tis clear that you have seen her not. The crown

    Is not more fair and joyous than she is

    Of beams a-flicker on yon lonely fir,

    Nor faeries in the honey-heart of June astir,

    By bosky June I swear, and by the bee, her minister.

NASCHINA: There is no way but that ye fight I wis,

    If *her* ye love.

THERNOT: Aye, Colin, we must fight.

COLIN: Aye, fight we must.

                [ANTONIO *and* NASCHINA *turn to go.*

 NASCHINA: Tell me, Antonio, might

    They get them swords, and both or either fall?

ANTONIO: No, no; when that shall be, then men may call

    Down to their feet the stars that shine alone,

    Each one at gaze for aye upon his whirling throne.

                    [*They go.*

(END OF SCENE I)

Scene II

*A remote part of the forest.—Through black and twisted trees
the lake is shining under the red evening sky.*

Enter NASCHINA *as a shepherd-boy, and* ANTONIO.

ANTONIO: Behold, how like a swarm of fiery bees
    The light is dancing o'er the knotted trees,
    In busy flakes; re-shining from the lake,
    Through this night-vested place the red beams break.
NASCHINA: From the deep earth unto the lurid sky
    All things are quiet in the eve's wide eye.
ANTONIO: The air is still above, and still each leaf,
    But loud the grasshopper that sits beneath.
NASCHINA: And, boy, we saw you, when through the forest we
    Two came, his name and mine on many a tree
    Carved; here, beyond the lake's slow-muffled tread
    In sand his name and mine I've also read.
ANTONIO: Yonder's the isle in search whereof we came;
    The white waves wrap it in a sheet of flame,

And yonder huddling blackness draweth nigh—
The faery ship that swims athwart the sky.

NASCHINA: Antonio, if I return no more,
Then bid them raise my statue on the shore;
Here where the round waves come, here let them build,
Here, facing to the lake, and no name gild;
A white, dumb thing of tears, here let it stand,
Between the lonely forest and the sand.

ANTONIO: The boat draws near and near. You heed me not!

NASCHINA: And when the summer's deep, then to this spot
The Arcadians bring, and bid the stone be raised
As I am standing now—as though I gazed,
One hand brow-shading, far across the night,
And one arm pointing thus, in marble white,
And once a-year let the Arcadians come,
And 'neath it sit, and of the woven sum
Of human sorrow let them moralize;
And let them tell sad histories, till their eyes
All swim with tears.

ANTONIO: The faery boat's at hand
You must be gone; the rolling grains of sand
Are 'neath its prow, and crushing shells.

NASCHINA [*turning to go*]: And let the tale be mournful each
one tells.

[ANTONIO *and* NASCHINA *go out.*

41

Re-enter ANTONIO.

ANTONIO: I would have gone also; but far away
  The faery thing flew with her o'er the grey
  Slow waters, and the boat and maiden sink
  Away from me where mists of evening drink
  To ease their world-old thirst along the brink
  Of sword-blue waves of calm; while o'er head blink
  The mobs of stars in gold and green and blue,
  Piercing the quivering waters through and through,
  The ageless sentinels who hold their watch
  O'er grief. The world drinks sorrow from the beams
  And penetration of their eyes.

           [*Starting forward.*

    Where yonder blotch
  Of lilac o'er the pulsing water gleams,
  Once more those shepherds come. Mayhap some mirth
  I'll have. Oh, absent one, 'tis not for dearth
  Of grief. And if they say, "Antonio laughed,"
  Say then,—"A popinjay before grief's shaft
  Pierced through, chattering from habit in the sun,
  Till his last wretchedness was o'er and done."

A VOICE FROM THE TREES: Antonio!

Enter COLIN *and* THERNOT.

THERNOT: We have resolved to fight.

ANTONIO: To yonder isle, where never sail was furled,

    From whose green banks no living thing may rove,

    And see again the happy woodland light,

    Naschina's gone, drawn by a thirst of love,

    And that was strange; but *this* is many a world

    More wonderful!

THERNOT: And we have swords.

ANTONIO: O night

    Of wonders! eve of prodigies!

COLIN: Draw! Draw!

ANTONIO (aside): He'll snap his sword.

THERNOT: Raised is the lion's paw.

COLIN *and* THERNOT *fight.*

ANTONIO: Cease! Thernot's wounded, cease! They will not heed.

    Fierce thrust! A tardy blossom had the seed,

    But heavy fruit. How swift the argument

    Of those steel tongues! Crash, swords! Well thrust! Well bent!

    Aside!—

                [A far-off multitudinous sound of horns.

    The wild horns told Almintor's end,

43

And of Naschina's now they tell—rend! rend!
Oh heart! Her dirge! With rushing arms the waves
Cast on the sound, on, on. This night of graves,
The spinning stars—the toiling sea—whirl round
My sinking brain! Cease! Cease! Heard ye yon sound?
The dirge of her ye love. Cease! Cease!

[*An echo in a cliff in the heart of the forest sends mournfully back the blast of the horns.* ANTONIO *rushes away, and the scene closes on* COLIN *and* THERNOT *still fighting.*]

(END OF SCENE II)

Scene III

THE ISLAND.—*Flowers of manifold colour are knee-deep before a gate of brass, above which, in a citron-tinctured sky, glimmer a few stars. At intervals come mournful blasts from the horns among the flowers.*

FIRST VOICE: What do you weave so fair and bright?

SECOND VOICE: The cloak I weave of sorrow.

    Oh, lovely to see in all men's sight

    Shall be the cloak of sorrow,

    In all men's sight.

THIRD VOICE: What do you build with sails for?

FOURTH VOICE: A boat I build for sorrow.

    O swift on the seas all day and night

    Saileth the rover sorrow,

    All day and night.

FIFTH VOICE: What do you weave with wool so white?

SIXTH VOICE: The sandals these of sorrow,

    Soundless shall be the footfall light

In each man's ears of sorrow,
Sudden and light.

NASCHINA, *disguised as a shepherd-boy, enters with
the* ENCHANTRESS, *the beautiful familiar of the Isle.*

NASCHINA: What are the voices that in flowery ways
    Have clothed their tongues with song of songless days?
ENCHANTRESS: They are the flowers' guardian sprights;
    With streaming hair as wandering lights
    They passed a-tip-toe everywhere,
    And never heard of grief or care
    Until this morn. As adder's back
    The sky was banded o'er with wrack.
    They were sitting round a pool,
    At their feet the waves in rings
    Gently shook their moth-like wings;
    For there came an air-breath cool
    From the ever-moving pinions
    Of the happy flower minions.
    But a sudden melancholy
    Filled them as they sat together;
    Now their songs are mournful wholly
    As they go with drooping feather.
NASCHINA: O, Lady, thou whose vestiture of green

Is rolled as verdant smoke! O thou whose face
Is worn as though with fire. Oh, goblin queen,
Lead me, I pray thee, to the statued place!

ENCHANTRESS: Fair youth, along a wandering way
I've led thee here, and as a wheel
We turned around the place always,
Lest on thine heart the stony seal
As on those other hearts were laid.
Behold the brazen-gated glade!

[*She partially opens the brazen gates; the statues are
seen within; some are bending, with their hands
among the flowers; others are holding withered flowers.*

NASCHINA: O let me pass! the spells from off the heart
Of my sad hunter-friend will all depart
If on his lips the enchanted flower be laid;
O let me pass!

[*Leaning with an arm upon each gate.*

ENCHANTRESS: That flower none
Who seek may find, save only one,
A shepherdess long years foretold;
And even she shall never hold
The flower save some thing be found
To die for her in air or ground.
And none there is; if such there were,
E'en then before her shepherd hair

Had felt the island breeze, my lore
Had driven her forth, for ever more
To wander by the bubbling shore.
Laughter-lipped, but for her brain
A guerdon of deep-rooted pain,
And in her eyes a lightless stare,
For if severed from the root
The enchanted flower were,
From my wizard island lair,
And the happy wingéd day,
I, as music that grows mute,
On a girl's forgotten lute,
Pass away—

NASCHINA: Your eyes are all a-flash. She is not here.

ENCHANTRESS: I d kill her if she were. Nay, do not fear!
With you I am all gentleness; in truth,
There's little I'd refuse thee, dearest youth.

NASCHINA: It is my whim! bid some attendant sprite
Of thine cry over wold and water white,
That one shall die, unless one die for her.
'Tis but to see if anything will stir
For such a call. Let the wild word be cried
As though she whom you fear had crossed the wide
Swift lake.

ENCHANTRESS: A very little thing that is,
And shall be done, if you will deign to kiss

My lips, fair youth.

NASCHINA: It shall be as you ask.

ENCHANTRESS: Forth! Forth! O spirits, ye have heard your task!

VOICES: We are gone!

ENCHANTRESS [*sitting down by* NASCHINA]:

Fair shepherd, as we wandered hither,

My words were all: "Here no loves wane and wither,

Where dream-fed passion is and peace encloses,

Where revel of fox-glove is and revel of roses."

My words were all: "O whither, whither, whither

Wilt roam away from this rich island rest?

I bid thee stay, renouncing thy mad quest."

But thou wouldst not, for then thou wert unblest

And stony-hearted; now thou hast grown kind,

And thou wilt stay. All thought of what they find

In the far world will vanish from thy mind,

Till thou rememberest only how the sea

Has fenced us round for all eternity.

But why art thou so silent? Did'st thou hear I laughed?

NASCHINA: And why is that a thing so dear?

ENCHANTRESS: From thee I snatched it; e'en the fay that trips

At morn, and with her feet each cobweb rends,

Laughs not. It dwells alone on mortal lips:

Thou'lt teach me laughing and I'll teach thee peace,

Here where laburnum hangs her golden fleece;

For peace and laughter have been seldom friends.

49

But for a boy how long thine hair has grown!
Long citron coils that hang around thee, blown
In shadowy dimness. To be fair as thee
I'd give my faery fleetness, though I be
Far fleeter than the million-footed sea.

A VOICE: By wood antique, by wave and waste,
Where cypress is and oozy pine,
Did I on quivering pinions haste,
And all was quiet round me spread,
As quiet as the clay-cold dead.
I cried the thing you bade me cry.
An owl, who in an alder tree
Had hooted for an hundred years,
Up-raised his voice, and hooted me.
E'en though his wings were plumeless stumps,
And all his veins had near run dry,
Forth from the hollow alder trunk
He hooted as I wandered by.
And so with wolf, and boar, and steer.
And one alone of all would hark,
A man who by a dead man stood.
A star-lit rapier, half blood-dark,
Was broken in his quivering hand.
As blossoms, when the winds of March
Hold festival across the land,
He shrank before my voice, and stood

Low bowed and dumb upon the sand.

A foolish word thou gavest me!

For each within himself hath all

The world, within his folded heart,

His temple and his banquet hall;

And who will throw his mansion down

Thus for another's bugle call!

ENCHANTRESS: But why this whim of thine? A strange unrest,

As alien as a cuckoo in a robin's nest,

Is in thy face, and lips together pressed;

And why so silent? I would have thee speak.

Soon wilt thou smile, for here the winds are weak

As moths with broken wings, and as we sit

The heavens all star-throbbing are a-lit.

NASCHINA: But art thou happy?

ENCHANTRESS: Let me gaze on thee

At arm's length, thus till dumb eternity

Has rolled away the stars and dried the sea

I could gaze, gaze upon thine eyes clear grey;

Gaze on till ragged time himself decay.

Ah! you are weeping here should all grief cease.

NASCHINA: But art thou happy?

ENCHANTRESS: Youth, I am at peace.

NASCHINA: But art thou happy?

ENCHANTRESS: Those grey eyes of thine,

Have they ne'er seen the eyes of lynx or kine,

Or aught remote; or hast thou never heard
Mid bubbling leaves a wandering song-rapt bird
Going the forest through, with flutings weak;
Or hast thou never seen, with visage meek,
A hoary hunter leaning on his bow,
To watch thee pass? Yet deeper than men know
These are at peace.

A VOICE: Sad lady, cease!
I rose, I rose
        From the dim wood's foundation—
I rose, I rose
        Where in white exultation
The long lily blows,
And the wan wave that lingers
        From flood-time encloses
With infantine fingers
        The roots of the roses.
Thence have I come winging;
        I there had been keeping
        A mouse from his sleeping,
With shouting and singing.

ENCHANTRESS: How sped thy quest? This prelude we'll not hear it
I' faith thou ever wast a wordy spirit!

THE VOICE: A wriggling thing on the white lake moved,
        As the canker-worm on a milk-white rose;
And down I came as a falcon swoops

When his sinewy wings together close.
I lit by the thing, 'twas a shepherd-boy,
　Who swimming sought the island lone;
Within his clenchéd teeth a sword.
　I heard the deathful monotone,
The water-serpent sings his heart
Before a death. O'er wave and bank
　I cried the words you bid me cry,
The shepherd raised his arms and sank,
　His rueful spirit fluttered by.

NASCHINA [*aside*]: I must bestir myself. Both dead for me!

Both dead!—No time to think.

[*Aloud*]　I am she,
　That shepherdess; arise and bring to me,
　In silence, that famed flower of wizardry,
　For I am mightier now by far than thee,
　And faded now is all thy wondrous art.

　　　　　　[*The* ENCHANTRESS *points to a cleft in a rock.*

NASCHINA: I see within a cloven rock dispart
　A scarlet bloom. Why raisest thou, pale one,
　Oh famous dying minion of the sun,
　Thy flickering hand? What mean the lights that rise
　As light of triumph in thy goblin eyes—
　In thy wan face?

ENCHANTRESS: Hear thou, O daughter of the days,
    Behold the loving loveless flower of lone ways,
    Well nigh immortal in this charméd clime,
    Thou shalt outlive thine amorous happy time,
    And dead as are the lovers of old rime
    Shall be the hunter-lover of thy youth.
    Yet ever more through all thy days of ruth,
    Shall grow thy beauty and thy dreamless truth,
    As an hurt leopard fills with ceaseless moan,
    And aimless wanderings the woodlands lone,
    Thy soul shall be, though pitiless and bright
    It is, yet shall it fail thee day and night
    Beneath the burthen of the infinite,
    In those far years, O daughter of the days.
    And when thou hast these things for many ages felt,
    The red squirrel shall rear her young where thou hast dwelt—
    Ah, woe is me! I go from sun and shade,
    And the joy of the streams where long-limbed herons wade;
    And never any more the wide-eyed bands
    Of the pied panther-kittens from my hands
    Shall feed. I shall not in the evenings hear
    Again the woodland laughter, and the clear
    Wild cries, grown sweet with lulls and lingerings long.
    I fade, and shall not see the mornings wake,
    A-fluttering the painted populace of lake
    And sedgy stream, and in each babbling brake

And hollow lulling the young winds with song.
I dream!—I cannot die!—No! no!
I hurl away these all unfaery fears.
Have I not seen a thousand seasons ebb and flow
The tide of stars? Have I not seen a thousand years
The summers fling their scents? Ah, subtile and slow,
The warmth of life is chilling, and the shadows grow
More dark beneath the poplars, where yon owl
Lies torn and rotting. The fierce kestrel birds
Slew thee, poor sibyl: comrades thou and I;
For, ah, our lives were but two starry words
Shouted a moment 'tween the earth and sky.
Oh death is horrible! and foul, foul, foul!

NASCHINA: I know not of the things you speak. But what
Of him on yonder brazen-gated spot,
By thee spell-bound?

ENCHANTRESS: Thou shalt know more:
Meeting long hence the phantom herdsman, king
Of the dread woods; along their russet floor
His sleuth-hounds follow every faery thing.

       [*Turns to go.* NASCHINA *tries to prevent her.*

Before I am too weak, fierce mortal, let me fly
And crouch in some far stillness of the isle, and die.

NASCHINA [*following*]: Will he have happiness? Great sobs her
being shake.

VOICES [*sing*]: A man has a hope for heaven,
        But soulless a faery dies,
  As a leaf that is old, and withered, and cold,
        When the wintry vapours rise.

Soon shall our wings be stilled,
        And our laughter over and done.
So let us dance where the yellow lance
        Of the barley shoots in the sun.

So let us dance on the fringéd waves,
        And shout at the wisest owls
In their downy caps, and startle the naps
        Of the dreaming water-fowls,

And fight for the black sloe-berries,
        For soulless a faery dies,
As a leaf that is old, and withered, and cold,
        When the wintry vapours rise.

                Re-enter NASCHINA.

NASCHINA: I plucked her backwards by her dress of green,
  To question her—oh no, I did not fear,
  Because St. Joseph's image hangeth here
  Upon my necklace. But the goblin queen
  Faded and vanished, nothing now is seen,

Saving a green frog dead upon the grass.

As figures moving mirrored in a glass,

The singing shepherds, too, have passed away .

O Arcady, O Arcady, this day

A deal of evil and of change hath crossed

Thy peace. Ah, now I'll wake these sleepers, lost

And woe-begone. For them no evil day!

[Throws open the brazen gates.

O wake! wake! wake! for soft as a bee sips

The faery flower lies upon thy lips.

ALMINTOR: I slept, 'twas sultry, and scarce circling

The falling hawthorn bloom. By mere and brook

The otters dreaming lay.

NASCHINA:　　Aye!

Behold the hapless sleepers standing by.

I will dissolve away the faeries' guile;

So be thou still, dear heart, a little while!

[To the Second Sleeper]

Old warrior, wake! for soft as a bee sips,

The faery blossom lies upon thy lips.

SLEEPER: Have I slept long?

NASCHINA:　　Long years.

THE SLEEPER:　　　With hungry heart

Doth still the Wanderer rove? With all his ships

I saw him from sad Dido's shores depart,

Enamoured of the waves' impetuous lips.

NASCHINA: Those twain are dust. Wake! Light as a bee sips

The faery blossom lies upon thy lips;

Seafarer, wake!

THIRD SLEEPER: Was my sleep long?

NASCHINA: Long years.

THE SLEEPER: A rover I, who come from where men's ears

Love storm; and stained with mist the new moons flare.

Doth still the Man whom each stern rover fears,

The austere Arthur rule from Uther's chair?

NASCHINA: He is long dead.

Wake! soft as a bee sips

The goblin flower lieth on thy lips

FOURTH SLEEPER: Was my sleep long, oh youth?

NASCHINA: Long, long and deep.

THE SLEEPER: As here I came I saw god Pan. He played

An oaten pipe unto a listening fawn,

Whose insolent eyes unused to tears would weep.

Doth he still dwell within the woody shade,

And rule the shadows of the eve and dawn?

NASCHINA: Nay, he is gone. Wake! wake! as a bee sips

The faery blossom broods upon thy lips.

Sleeper, awake!

FIFTH SLEEPER: How long my sleep?

NASCHINA: Unnumbered

The years of goblin sleep.

THE SLEEPER: Ah! while I slumbered,

    How have the years in Troia flown away?

    Are still the Achaians' tented chiefs at bay?

    Where rise the walls majestical above

    The plain, a little fair-haired maid I love.

THE SLEEPERS ALL TOGETHER: She is long ages dust.

THE SLEEPER: Ah, woe is me!

FIRST SLEEPER: Youth, here will we abide, and be thou king

    Of this lake-nurtured isle.

NASCHINA: Let thy king be

    Yon archer, he who hath the halcyon's wing

    As flaming minstrel-word upon his crest

ALL THE SLEEPERS : Clear-browed Arcadian, thou shalt be our king!

NASCHINA: O, my Almintor, noble was thy quest;

    Yea, noble and most knightly hath it been.

ALL THE SLEEPERS : Clear-browed Arcadian, thou shalt be our king.

ALMINTOR: Until we die within the charmed ring

    Of these star-shuddering skies you are the queen.

[*The rising moon casts the shadows of* ALMINTOR *and the Sleepers far across the grass. Close by* ALMINTOR's *side* NASCHINA *is standing, shadowless.*

THE END

The Seeker

A Dramatic Poem—In Two Scenes

Scene I

A woodland valley at evening. Around a wood-fire sit three shepherds; without a curve rises the smoke.

FIRST SHEPHERD: Heavy with wool the sheep are gathered in,
    And through the mansion of the spirit rove
    My dreams o'er thoughts of plenty, as the red-
    Eyed panthers in their desert caverns rove
    And rove unceasing round their dreadful brood.
SECOND SHEPHERD: O brother, lay thy flute upon thy lips,
    It is the voice of all our hearts that laugh.

                [The first Shepherd puts the flute to his lips;
                there comes from it a piercing cry. He drops it.
FIRST SHEPHERD: It is possessed.

THIRD SHEPHERD: Nay, give it me, and I will sound a measure;
　　And unto it we'll dance upon the sward.
　　[*Puts it to his lips. A voice out of the flute still more mournful.*
FIRST SHEPHERD: An omen!
SECOND SHEPHERD: An omen!
THIRD SHEPHERD: A creeping horror is all over me.

Enter an OLD KNIGHT. *They cast themselves down before him.*

KNIGHT: Are all things well with you and with your sheep?
SECOND SHEPHERD: Yes, all is very well.
FIRST SHEPHERD:　Whence comest thou?
KNIGHT: Shepherds, I came this morning to your land
　　From threescore years of dream-led wandering
　　Where spice-isles nestle on the star-trod seas
　　And where the polar winds and waters wrestle
　　In endless dark, and by the weedy marge
　　Of India's rivers, rolling on in light.
　　But soon my wandering shall be done, I know.
　　A voice has told me how within this land
　　There lies the long-lost forest of the sprite,
　　The sullen wood. But many woods I see
　　Where to themselves innumerable birds
　　Make moan and cry.
FIRST SHEPHERD:　Within yon sunless valley

Between the horned hills—

KNIGHT: Shepherds, farewell!

And peace be with you, peace and wealth of days.

SECOND SHEPHERD: Seek not that wood, for there the goblin snakes

Go up and down, and raise their heads and sing

With little voices songs of fearful things.

THIRD SHEPHERD: No shepherd foot has ever dared its depths.

FIRST SHEPHERD: The very squirrel dies that enters it.

KNIGHT: Shepherds, farewell!

[*Goes.*

SECOND SHEPHERD: He soon will be—

FIRST SHEPHERD: Ashes

Before the wind.

THIRD SHEPHERD: Saw you his eyes a-glitter,

His body shake?

SECOND SHEPHERD: Aye, quivering as yon smoke

That from the fire is ever pouring up,

Within the woodways blue as the halcyon's wing,

Star-envious.

THIRD SHEPHERD: He was a spirit, brother.

SECOND SHEPHERD: The blessed God was good to send us such,

To make us glad with wonder as we sat

Weary of watching round the fire at night.

(END OF SCENE I)

SCENE II

A ruined palace in the forest. Away in the depth of the shadow of
the pillars a motionless FIGURE.

Enter the OLD KNIGHT.

KNIGHT: Behold I bend before thee to the ground
    Until my beard is in the twisted leaves
    That with their fiery ruin fill the hall,
    As words of thine through fourscore years have filled
    My echoing heart. Now raise thy voice and speak!
    Even from boyhood, in my father's house,
    That was beside the waterfall, thy words
    Abode, as banded adders in my breast.
    Thou knowest this, and how from 'mid the dance
    Thou called'st me forth.

                And how thou madest me
    A coward in the field; and all men cried:
    Behold the Knight of the Waterfall, whose heart
    The spirits stole, and gave him in its stead

A peering hare's; and yet I murmured not,
Knowing that thou hadst singled me with word
Of love from out a dreamless race for strife,
Through miseries unhuman ever on
To joys unhuman, and to thee—Speak! Speak!

> [*He draws nearer to the* FIGURE. *A pause.*

Behold I bend before thee to the ground;
Thou wilt not speak, and I with age am near
To Death. His lips are glued, with quivering touch,
To mine, and he is slowly sucking forth
My soul. His darkness and his chill I feel.
Were all my wandering days of no avail
Untouched of human joy or human love?
Then let me see thy face before I die.
Behold I bow before thee to the ground!
Behold I bow! Around my beard in drifts
Lie strewn the clotted leaves—the dead old leaves.

> [*He gathers up the leaves and presses them to his breast.*

Thou wilt not speak, Oh cruel art thou yet!
Mine heart-strings are all broken saving one,
That trembles and resounds with hymns to thee,
That fill the blazing hollows of my heart.
I'm dying. Oh forgive me if I touch
Thy garment's hem, thou visionary one!

[*He approaches close to the* FIGURE. *A sudden light bursts over it.*

KNIGHT: A bearded witch her sluggish head low bent

On her broad breast! beneath her withered brows

Shine dull unmoving eyes. What thing art thou?

I sought thee not.

FIGURE: Men call me Infamy.

I know not what I am.

KNIGHT: I sought thee not.

FIGURE: Lover, the voice that summoned thee was mine.

KNIGHT: For all I gave the voice, for all my youth,

For all my joy—Ah woe!

[*The* FIGURE *raises a mirror in which the face*

and the form of the Knight are shadowed.

He falls forward.

FIGURE [*bending over him, and speaking in his ear*]:

What! Lover, die before our lips have met?

KNIGHT: Again, the voice! the voice!

[*Dies.*

THE END

The Song of
the Happy Shepherd

An Epilogue

to THE ISLAND OF STATUES and THE SEEKER

[*Spoken by a Satyr carrying a sea-shell.*]

The woods of Arcady are dead,
And over is their antique joy;
Of old the world on dreaming fed;
Grey Truth is now her painted toy;
Yet still she turns her restless head:
But O, sick children of the world,
Of all the many changing things
In dreary dancing past us whirled,
To the cracked tune that Chronos sings,
Words alone are certain good.
Where are now the warring kings,
Word be-mockers?—By the Rood,
Where are now the warring kings?

An idle word is now their glory,
By the stammering schoolboy said,
Reading some entangled story:
The kings of the old time are dead;
The wandering earth herself may be
Only a sudden flaming word,
In clanging space a moment heard,
Troubling the endless reverie.

Then nowise worship dusty deeds,
Nor seek, for this is also sooth,
To hunger fiercely after truth,
Lest all thy toiling only breeds
New dreams, new dreams; there is no truth
Saving in thine own heart. Seek, then,
No learning from the starry men,
Who follow with the optic glass
The whirling ways of stars that pass—
Seek, then, for this is also sooth,
No word of theirs—the cold star-bane
Has cloven and rent their hearts in twain,
And dead is all their human truth.
Go gather by the humming sea
Some twisted, echo-harbouring shell,
And to its lips thy story tell,
And they thy comforters will be,

Rewording in melodious guile
Thy fretful words a little while,
Till they shall singing fade in ruth
And die a pearly brotherhood;
For words alone are certain good:
Sing, then, for this is also sooth.

I must be gone: there is a grave
Where daffodil and lily wave,
And I would please the hapless faun,
Buried under the sleepy ground,
With mirthful songs before the dawn.
His shouting days with mirth were crowned;
And still I dream he treads the lawn,
Walking ghostly in the dew,
Pierced by my glad singing through,
My songs of old earth's dreamy youth:
But ah! she dreams not now; dream thou!
For fair are poppies on the brow:
Dream, dream, for this is also sooth.

ABOUT THE AUTHOR

William Butler Yeats was born in Dublin in 1865, and educated in Ireland and England. He published numerous volumes of poetry, initially influenced by the Romantics and Pre-Raphaelites, and later by Symbolism. He was deeply involved in the Irish liberation movement, and after Ireland's independence served as a senator for two terms. Yeats was awarded the 1923 Nobel Prize in Literature.

CPSIA information can be obtained
at www.ICGtesting.com
Printed in the USA
LVOW10s0413200218
567229LV00001B/102/P